SANCTUARY

SANCTUARY

Unexpected Places Where God Found Me

Becca Stevens

DIMENSIONS
FOR LIVING
NASHVILLE

SANCTUARY
UNEXPECTED PLACES WHERE GOD FOUND ME

Copyright © 2005 by Dimensions for Living

This book is printed on acid-free paper.

Library of Congress Cataloging-in-Publication Data

Stevens, Becca, 1963–
    Sanctuary : unexpected places where God found me / Becca
Stevens.
        p. cm.
    ISBN 0-687-49420-6 (pbk. : alk. paper)
    1. Meditations.   2. Stevens, Becca, 1963–   .   I. Title.
    BV4832.3.S74 2005
    242—dc22

                                                    2005015053

All scripture quotations are taken from the *New Revised Standard
Version of the Bible*, copyright © 1989, by the Division of Christian
Education of the National Council of the Churches of Christ in the
United States of America. Used by permission. All rights reserved.

05 06 07 08 09 10 11 12 13 14—10 9 8 7 6 5 4 3 2 1
MANUFACTURED IN THE UNITED STATES OF AMERICA

CONTENTS

INTRODUCTION

THE FOLLOWING MEDITATIONS DESCRIBE PLACES OF
sanctuary I have found in my life. They are spaces
and moments of grace that I have tried my best to
record over the past several years. A couple are
funny, a few are poetic, some are peaceful, and
probably too many are fragmented. They are
offered in honor of all the times I have forgotten to
see the clouds parting or the vision clearing. These
meditations on sanctuaries are the result of a long
journey gladly taken on the side roads. Sanctuary is
an ideal that speaks to our souls. It is one of the
greatest gifts that religion has offered humanity
throughout history. It offers pilgrims respite, peace,
and hope as they journey in this world. It is a non-
violent endeavor that extends beyond any borders
created by nations or religious institutions. When I
think of sanctuary, I often think of places of worship that people have blessed specifically for that
purpose. I think of places I have worshiped as a
child and places that from a distance seemed to
embody the meaning of sanctuary. I think of places
such as the churches in Arizona where illegal immi-
grants were granted protection from law enforce-
ment in the 1970s; or in Lourdes, France, where

sick pilgrims come from all over the world to bathe in healing waters. I think of chapels where the Civil Rights movement was born and raised and amazing altars where saints have been carved from marble to inspire us to live up to the highest ideals of our faith. But I have also learned to find sanctuary in nature, in jails, in my home, and in places I had forgotten to look.

The meditations begin and end with poems depicting sanctuaries I found on the Cumberland Plateau in Sewanee, Tennessee. It is fitting for me to begin and end there, as both my parents are buried in a small cemetery in the middle of the college campus on that plateau. It is where I went to college and where I have continued to go to hike and spend days in silence. It is a place that is close to home and that helps me remember what it means to pray.

Some of the sanctuaries are churches, where I have sat in silence and tried to feel how the space is speaking to my spirit. Most are simply places that came as beautiful surprises on the way to somewhere else. They are a witness to the truth that in our lives of faith, it is in the journey, not in the destination, where we learn what it means to love God with our whole heart and to love our neighbors.

To be able to experience sanctuary in this world is not being sentimental and ignoring the real pain and suffering of others. It is not being simplistic and ignoring the myriad of layers reflected in the scenes I have described. It is being courageous enough to name love as real and palpable in every place we walk. It is being optimistic in believing that love can be a powerful force for change in the world. And it is being faithful to the promise of a God who made the world sacramental by sending love to be incarnate among us. I hope that in reading these meditations you are inspired to look again at your surroundings and see God's love and presence filling your days.

ACKNOWLEDGMENTS

FOR THE PAST DECADE I HAVE SERVED AS EPISCOPAL Chaplain at St. Augustine's Chapel on Vanderbilt University campus. St. Augustine's is a vibrant and humble place where about three hundred people gather to worship and work together. It has been a wonderful place for me to search out my heart and learn how to lead a community of faith. The congregation at the chapel makes it easy to see how the practice of including everyone without judgment makes loving God a joy.

I have also served as the founder and executive director of Magdalene, a two-year residential program for women with a criminal history of prostitution and drug abuse, begun in 1997. We now have four houses and serve twenty-five women at any given time. We take no federal or state money and run our four houses loosely according to the old Benedictine practice of a common rule for living. From its inception, Magdalene has been envisioned as a gift to the women, the staff, and the community we serve. It embodies the ideal that one of the best things that a community can offer is sanctuary from the world. In February 2001, we started a cottage industry called Thistle Farms that makes bath and body care products. Thistle Farms currently has fourteen employees and approximately fifty volunteers who help generate $200,000 annually in revenue for Magdalene.

Thank you to my friends at St. Augustine's and Magdalene, and to you for taking the time to read these meditations.

Becca Stevens

Before the sun rose
Or an altar was hewn
Before the crocus bloomed
Or a winter passed

Before the birds sang
Or the seas parted
Before a word was spoken
Or an apple bitten

Before the wine was blessed
Or a cross lifted
Before the path was chosen
Or a prayer offered

There was sanctuary.

KROGER PARKING LOT

IT ALL BEGAN TO COME TOGETHER SITTING IN THE KROGER parking lot on Nolensville Road one bright, sunny day in May. I sat for about half an hour in my car in silence and watched the people coming in and going out of the grocery. There was a man who looked exactly like an usher assisting people with their groceries. He wore a hearing aid in each ear and talked the whole time he was pushing carts. There were about twenty hanging baskets, arranged by the grocery-store version of the altar guild, and hundreds of people coming to get their bread to break. It felt truthful and practical, and I loved watching the lot being used for such a wholesome activity.

This ground was, literally, my father's house of prayer. Before it was a supermarket parking lot, it held the church where my father preached for two years before he died in an auto accident at the age of forty-one. On this lot was an old white house that served as a parish hall, as well as a more recent church that was built in the 1960s. The church probably had a hundred members when my father died. After his death, my mom and all five of her children continued to live in the rectory nearby and go to services there. That church was the place where I

learned to pray and learned that casseroles are good medicine for grief. It was also the place where I was sexually molested by the senior warden in the upstairs of the fellowship hall during a spaghetti supper and where I learned to smoke cigarettes.

It is amazing to look back from this vantage point thirty-five years later and feel God's mercy all along the way. There is no regret, just compassion for all the people involved. I remember hearing that when the congregation decided to sell the church, they held a service to deconsecrate the sanctuary. I remember thinking that it was a waste of time. The church was desecrated years before in that fellowship hall.

On the same site in 1981, just as I was leaving town to head out on my own, the supermarket was built, and it seemed right and holy and useful to build a place where people will actually be fed. Sitting here I can see people who look like they come from every station in life, and they are coming to be fed, not judged. I love sitting here and remembering that from this place I grew a heart for faith and for communities that offer sanctuary to everybody in the whole wide world.

DIVING IN SECRET WATERS

THERE IS A POND HIDDEN DOWN A GRAVEL ROAD OFF Tyne Boulevard, near a stand of hackberries. We swam there as children, but now it is being divided into five lots, and so this may be the last time I get to drive into this hidden paradise. Cars pass by all day long and never know that just beyond the scrim of kudzu and honeysuckle lie the coolest and clearest spring waters known, tucked away like a secret Eden.

When we were kids we would bike over, run up the gravel road, swing open the vine-covered gate, jump down three huge slabs of rock, and run past the elms and oaks that served as the perimeter of our paradise. The enormous pool of water was a part of the landscape and contained long steps, meandering shallows, and wondrous deep hollows to explore. You couldn't see a house or hear a car from that pool.

The water itself was freezing. We would step forward, inch by inch, until the stinging subsided and it was more painful to stay above the water. Then we would dive in, free from every bit of summer's sticky, buggy, humid air, lost in the cool waters that healed us from boredom, envy, pride, bitterness, depression, or anything else that could hold a spirit down.

These are the secret waters that are offered to us all, untapped by the people who drive by, focused on trying to get to a place where the grass is greener. As we approach, we push aside the kudzu, the shame, and the guilt. We step past the hackberries to a place beyond fairness and revenge, to a place of sanctuary.

Once inside, we negotiate the sandstone slabs while humming in our head the mantra from our youth, "Forgive us our trespasses as we forgive those who trespass against us." As we jump down the steps, we ponder forgiveness—that it is perfected in the infinite, that it is inversely proportional to the transgression, that it is an attribute of God. We remember that forgiving doesn't lessen the power of the events in our lives; it doesn't make others unaccountable, nor does it make us unaccountable. But with each step we surrender our need to have an accounting or to remain victims, so that we can release our resentment and dive in freely.

If we can remember all that, we can stand at the shallows of the inviting waters. No other path takes us down to this paradise—not power, not begging, not wishing. The mysterious waters call us despite reason and the impossibility of swimming in such an amazing pool. And we find miraculously that the waters, despite the initial sting, are indeed paradise. In them we are free to explore our hearts, weightless in our search for the deep places of our souls, and we let the waters take us under and wash us clean.

A REUNION IN JAIL

I REMEMBER THE FIRST TIME I VISITED A JAIL.

I had told an attorney friend of mine that I was interested in visiting jails and talking with the women prisoners, even though I had absolutely no experience at it. One day he called to say that a woman who had gone to high school with us was in jail for using drugs. He asked if I'd like to go with him to see her, and I said yes.

When we got to the jail, we discovered that one of the policemen there had also gone to high school with us. He and I were extremely surprised to see each other in our new roles.

"I can't believe you're a policeman," I said. "Don't they run background checks anymore?"

"You think that's hard to believe," Tom replied. "Who actually let you be a priest?"

We both laughed and I told him I was there to see our friend. He said he had heard that from one of the jail counselors, who had also gone to our high school and had called to let him know I was coming.

The prisoner, the priest, the policeman, the attorney, and the counselor were having a reunion, fourteen years and four miles away from our alma mater. Knowing everyone in that reunion circle, seeing how closely we were connected, I saw how easily we could have switched roles.

Going to the jail that day taught me that the lines separating us are infinitely small and that what we do for one another, we really do for ourselves. It was the beginning of my efforts to help women coming off the streets and out of jail, though it would be several years before I opened the first home called Magdalene.

I was nervous walking into the jail that day, but I have since had many experiences of God in that place. Jail calls us to find God and one another in whatever circle and circumstance we find ourselves. When Jesus stood up in the temple at the beginning of his ministry, he read the scripture that said he had come to set the captives free. Jail is like a concrete beatitude: Blessed are the prisoners, for they know freedom.

SHADES OF BROWN
IN BOTSWANA

MY FAMILY HAD BEEN TRAVELING IN BOTSWANA FOR almost three weeks, and we were headed toward the South African border to go on a safari. We had been driving for about six hours and were feeling pretty lost.

Botswana was a lesson that life is not black and white, but a thousand shades of brown. There was the brown of the grasses and trees, the brown of the dirt and houses, the brown of fur and skin. Even the shadows and sky were brown.

Levi, my firstborn, had been asking us for days to play his Led Zeppelin CD. Driving down this wide dirt road where elephants roamed free, we finally acquiesced, and the sounds of classic rock filled the air with strange background music. The very moment the lead guitarist, Jimmy Page, was beginning his legendary solo on track number four, a Botswanan teenager emerged from the bush like a star in a music video. He was lost in his own world, holding a handmade guitar and rocking out. From our vantage point it appeared as if he were in fact playing the solo from the CD live.

The teenager's guitar was made from an old

antifreeze bottle with a wooden neck nailed to it. Attached to the neck were frets, tuning pins, and a harmonic device made from a soda can. There were only three strings remaining from the original five, but that didn't seem to bother the young man as he played against a backdrop of brush and deep brown earth.

Feeling drawn to the scene, we slowed down and turned the car around, watching as he continued to make music for himself and God. My husband, a musician, got out of the car and walked over to the young man with his own guitar. They spoke a little and then played each other's guitars. As I watched, I realized that they really were trading guitars.

All of a sudden I felt like I was watching a lesson in truth. The truth was coming not in startling black and white, but in this scene of gentle browns, which now included the brown of dust and guitars. Truth is beautiful and inspiring. Truth is homemade, and we have to go seek it out and recognize its subtleties. Real truth lives beyond politics and economics. It celebrates life and beauty and calls us to humility when we are given the gift to recognize it. In the end, truth will teach us that we are enough.

THE FROG JUMPS FOR JOY

THEY HAD ASKED ME TO COME AND PERFORM THEIR wedding months before, when it had sounded like a great idea to take off on a Saturday and drive a couple of hours on my own and preside at the wedding, then take a hike and head home. I had had no idea that it was going to be such a busy week or that I wouldn't have time to pull the service together.

When I got to the site there were probably a hundred people who had come and spent the night and were so excited to be a part of the wedding. "I think I'll take a walk before the wedding begins," I said to the bride, thinking that now that I had seen the beautiful place and the people I would be inspired to think of something to say to them.

I had walked down a wooded path for just a few minutes when a big green frog hopped into the middle of it. All at once a bigger black snake came out of nowhere and put the whole frog into its mouth. I couldn't help exclaiming, "Oh, Lord!" The startled snake stopped and turned toward me. It was that small turn that enabled the frog to leap from the snake's mouth. The frog hopped away as fast as it could, literally jumping for joy.

There are probably a million ways to look at that small event and feel God's presence in it. For me it was like the passage from Isaiah that says we will go out in joy and the trees will clap their hands. On those great and happy days, sometimes it feels like all of creation can celebrate with you. The frogs leap for joy, the clouds dance, and we are thankful just to be alive.

BEGGING FROM BEGGARS

I WAS DRIVING DOWN DICKERSON ROAD, A STREET NOTO-rious for prostitutes, looking for a woman I had known for a couple of years in the Magdalene program who had relapsed and lost everything. I was worried about her and wanted to tell her that if she ever wanted to come home to Magdelene, she was welcome. She had given the program so much in the year and a half that she had been in the community, I wanted to make sure she knew that we still loved her.

I saw her and parked the car. Recognizing me, she crossed four lanes of traffic to get to me. She asked if I had some money I could lend her, and just for a moment I got a glimpse of how desperate she was and how that street was a walking hell for her. I couldn't imagine trying to survive there. I asked her, "What is keeping you alive?" She told me it had got-ten so bad that she was begging from beggars. She said I might be surprised that beggars can be mighty sympathetic and generous. It made perfect sense that those who know what desperation feels like are willing to help someone else who is desperate.

I stood there with her, unwilling to give her money to use on crack, but wanting to be with her.

I knew that I was saying good-bye for at least a long time and that probably the best I could hope for was that she would be arrested before she was killed. I told her as honestly as I could that she was like a prodigal daughter and that that set her firmly in the Gospels near the heart of God. I told her I didn't understand exactly how, but that through her I had learned about grace. Then I said good-bye, believing that grace would be enough for her, and for me.

A WOMAN IN THE ANDES

I WAS TRAVELING WITH A GROUP ON A MISSION TRIP, AND we had taken a break from our drive through a forest in the Andes. We had stopped for lunch. Our van was parked by a gravel road with an old stone fence that protected us from the steep drop just past the shoulder.

We walked around, stretching our legs and taking in the sight of steep hills floating in the midst of clouds. I leaned over the small stone wall, and there she was—a woman hanging clothing over a tree limb in front of a small bamboo hut. The hut was quite a distance from the road, across a valley and partway up the mountain facing us. There were no visible paths leading to the hut, nor were any other huts within sight. There was only the woman and a forest full of trees.

I watched her move, trying to imagine how she got there and what she did during endless days and nights with no electricity. A question crept into my head: if a woman is alone in a forest and laughs but no one hears it, does she really make a sound? The question wove its way into my heart and touched one of my fears. I continued to watch the woman, sensing that somehow her presence was of great importance to me. I realized that the first question was part of a larger one: if a person lives her life without fame, without fortune, without even a witness, does it have meaning?

I knew that the answer was yes, but that didn't stop the question from frightening me. How would I make meaning in my life living completely alone in the wilderness? How do I make my life meaningful, knowing that I am not so different from that woman?

I learned from the woman on the hillside that when a tree falls in the forest, it always makes a sound because God, who created the tree and loves the world, will always hear it. When she laughs alone on the hillside, God laughs with her.

There was so much meaning in that woman's life that she spared a bit for me. I will never forget her or all that she taught me about what real relationships look like when we are alone before God. Life is more than the sum of its parts; it is the journey of the heart that begins with God and is returning to God.

BATHING MOSES

I GAVE MY SON MOSES A BATH. ALL MY BEST AND MOST hopeful thoughts for a meaningful and good life were washing over him as freely as the water. He was two months old, beautiful and round, healthy and strong. My heart had already broken and had made room for him to be in its center.

As I filled my hand with water once again, the thought crossed my mind, "Am I baptizing my son by accident?" If the act of baptism is the pouring of water on the forehead of a child of God by a minister of the church with prayers of love and encouragement and hope for eternal life, the answer was a definite yes. In fact, I decided I had baptized him about twenty times since his birth. I laughed to myself, thinking how silly the idea was. "I'm just his mom," I said to no one. "I'm just giving him a bath."

And with the ideas of baths and baptism floating in my mind, I begin a journey along the mother line, imagining countless women with no authority, baptizing their babies with handfuls of bath water and prayers. Alone with their babies, they are free to celebrate and marvel at their children's specialness As if turning the pages of a huge photo

album, I leaf through generations of mothers bathing all sorts and conditions of babies—healthy ones, sick ones, crying ones, boys and girls, all races and creeds, each baby perfect to the new mother whose heart is just mending and who offers prayers of love as she washes the new skin.

I see a mother in the Middle Ages, bathing a newborn and then buttoning up the baby's home-tatted dress so the priest can come and pour a bit of water on her head and wipe it off quickly as it begins to drip. I see a rural woman waiting months for the itinerant preacher to come, and then rushing and quickly cleaning the baby so the prayers can begin and the feast commence. And I see myself rushing to the hospital the previous year to baptize a dying baby whose mother has already wept a river of tears on his forehead, giving that infant the most holy bath of all. I see each of these women beaming with pride, thankful that others have truly joined in all her silent prayers for the baby.

And, in my heart, I see that I, too, will dress my son in a beautiful gown and take him to the church to be blessed in front of the whole community that I love. I will introduce my son to the sacrament of baptism as I bathe him with every good thing that I know. I want the community of faith to promise to love him and care for him. Then I will take him home and continue to bathe him, with one handful of water at a time, whispering prayers of grace and love, and showering him with kisses.

LEVITATING IN MY OFFICE

IF I TOLD ANYONE THAT YESTERDAY I WAS LEVITATING IN my office, they probably would think I was crazy. But I swear that is what it felt like.

I had a meeting that morning with two women from Magdalene's staff who disagreed about how we should work. We all had decided it was going to be best to talk it out and make some decisions. I had thought long and hard about the meeting before I stepped into it, especially since my role was to act as arbitrator and help some final decisions be made. I had decided we should start with a few moments of silence so that we could all just relax a little in the space and be present. Then my plan was to say little, allowing the women to express themselves and speak freely.

Now, my office is cluttered with stuff from church and from Magdalene. It's really just an eight-by-ten-foot concrete monastic cell. It has one window that looks out onto a sidewalk that is home to a soda machine. I have never felt particularly inspired or oppressed by this space; I just use it for utilitarian purposes and sometimes think of what I would do with more room.

The women walked in, and they agreed to begin

with a few moments of silence. I said I would call us into the meeting afterwards. They agreed, and with eyes closed I took some deep breaths and thought about how I wanted this space to be filled with compassion and mercy. Then I am not sure what happened.

Some time went by, and the air seemed thick, as if it would have taken a tremendous amount of strength not just to speak, but to move a muscle at all. At the same time I felt euphoric and filled up with lightness in my being. I thought briefly that I should say something, but I could not bring myself to wake up out of that state to speak.

The next thing I remember was that I was watching the three of us in prayer from the vantage point of the ceiling. I could see all of us being reverent and silent, but viewing from above I thought how sad it was that we stay confined in our bodies all the time.

The other thing I remember that morning was that I had to jerk myself awake, almost like when you know you are asleep but need to get up and it takes all your effort. Somehow it made me sad. I pulled myself back together, almost literally it seemed, and lifted my heavy eyelids.

I said, "Thank you both for bringing the balance

of the spirit into this space. I think some people never get to feel that. I am in debt to both of you."

After that I think they talked and worked it all out until the next time, but I can't remember exactly what they worked out.

A BAPTISM OF TEARS

THIS WEEK I SAT WITH A YOUNG MOTHER I DIDN'T KNOW as doctors unplugged the machines attached to her eight-day-old son. I had walked into a room full of staff and family, as well as machines and tubes that were all set up to keep this baby alive. It had become clear in the last couple of days that it would be impossible to keep the baby going, and they had sent for me, a friend of a friend, to baptize the baby and be there as the doctors unplugged the machines.

The atmosphere inside the room was of complete reverence for this beautiful boy. He lay naked on a tall table with a heat lamp over him. He looked well, except for all the tubes that were pumping blood and oxygen for him. His mother and father had been keeping a vigil for days, and anyone coming through that door was brought into their mourning, so that the room was filled with prayer and an ageless sadness.

The mother asked me to baptize her son. She stroked his head. Her tears continued to fall, and I used them to make the sign of the cross on the baby's forehead. Then the doctors removed the machines. In a few hours the baby would die. Part of what made me so sad was thinking that the mother would still have to heal from the birth and that her milk would be there the next day and during the funeral. I tried to imagine the parents leaving this room and realizing that only about twenty people on earth had ever met their son.

I saw that the doctors and nurses were crying, as were the technicians and every other person in the room. Knowing that the professionals were grieving allowed some of us on the edges of the room not to be ashamed by our tears. There was a freedom in being allowed to grieve the baby and honor the parents, so we did. We stood in silence and cried while the mother and father whispered their love and farewells to their firstborn son.

ODE TO THE COMMON DEER

I HEARD A WILDLIFE EXPERT CALL A DEER A SQUIRREL, meaning that they were common and weren't worthy of our attention. So this morning, when a deer crossed my path by a field of larkspur, I took no notice of it. The scene before me was just plain common: a common deer running through a common field of wildflowers on a common day.

We have several common wildflowers in our state: there is the common daisy, the common daffodil, and then the horribly common dandelion. A few weeks ago my third son, Moses, came upon a group of dandelions in a field. It was right before the rains came. The wind picked up, and the dandelions began to dance about, nodding their white feather caps in the wind. Moses, not knowing that dandelions are common, nodded his head and began to dance with them.

One of the most common things on earth is a human being. Last I heard there were 6.5 billion of us, and yet we celebrate when there is one birth, mourn the loss of one person, marvel when one woman stays clean and sober from durgs. What can

be seen as common and ordinary to some can be special and wondrous to others. The difference is love. An ordinary lightning bolt was, to Saul, a revelation on the Road to Damascus. Just another fishing trip became a holy encounter with Jesus.

Now I long to see the deer in the field of larkspur, but it has long since gone. I give thanks for the common deer, the common grass aflame with larkspur, the common person thinking common thoughts in the uncommon world that God has created.

INSIDE IN

A FEW YEARS AGO, MY HUSBAND AND I WERE IN THE little town of Bread Loaf, Vermont, for a wedding. It was a beautiful October weekend, and the leaves were glorious. We stayed in a small house near a cabin where, for several years, Robert Frost wrote. After arriving, we went on a long walk through the woods, then went inside Frost's cabin to get a glimpse of his private life and breathe a bit of his discarded air.

We were moving about in silence through the cabin when we heard a padlock hit the door from the outside and then noticed the group happily walking down the path into the woods. I laughed, realizing that we were locked from the outside in. Since it was going to take a while for the group to realize we were missing and come back, I had some time to think.

Most of the time we view life from the inside out. From behind our interior walls we peer out and take in what we can see. This may work well for poets, but for most of us, looking from the inside out is too safe a place from which to view the truth. From this vantage point, when we look into the spiritual well for the image of Christ, we almost always find our own reflection. Standing behind our comfortable walls and drinking from our wells, we miss the truth.

Sometimes the truth is clearer when we look from the outside in. In this way we can use all the lessons of life, not to judge others, but to reexamine ourselves. We can go to a place of insight where nature and God speak to us and call us to break our familiar walls and stand exposed. Saint Theresa of Avila wrote that only then can we build our interior castles, with love as a foundation. From this vantage point all of life is a lesson that leaves us with humility and gratitude.

But there is still another way of looking at life. Beyond the inside out and the outside in, there is a deeper place that we might call the inside in. This is the place of dreams, the place where we touch the eternal. It is what the prophet Isaiah described as the holiest place, where mountains are leveled and iron doors are smashed. It is the place where there is no safety, where the treasures of darkness live. And when, every now and then, we move into this place, we can hear God, who has called us since birth, speaking our name.

The winter before Frost moved into this cabin,

his wife died, and the next summer his son killed himself. During those lost times, when his biographer described him as "a ship between jagged rocks," Robert Frost found a holy place looking from the inside in.

THE PLANETS LINE UP

THE BUILDING HAD BEEN FRAMED OUT AND THE WALLS were starting to go up. We had been working for about two years to build this residence for women coming off the street. We had raised a million dollars and had chosen to build it in a neighborhood in which drug dealers and prostitutes walk the streets. We were excited and full of apprehension and questions.

And so on a Thursday evening, about twelve friends decided to go over and pray silently in this space that was the newest home to many of our hopes and dreams. It was a little awkward at first, but soon we settled among the beams, in what was going to be the main living room. We started our silent prayer, with the sounds of the neighborhood all around.

What we didn't know was that in really poor neighborhoods, especially on the dead-end streets, they don't have any streetlights. What that means is that it is a great place for seeing the stars. It kind of surprised everyone, and you could feel people shuffling around to get a better view of the sky. Pretty soon the prayer wasn't being prayed with heads bowed and eyes closed. People were lifting their heads with their eyes wide open.

One of the really smart nursing school students who had been a volunteer during the project broke the silence, saying, "Look, there are Venus, Mars, and Saturn, all in a perfect line." The contractor on the house added, "I read about it but didn't think I would get to see it." I couldn't believe it. There we were, not just sitting under a canopy of stars on a deep clear night, but seeing all the planets line up.

Sometimes the most holy and magical moments for me are the ones between the vision and the coming true, between the hoping and the living it all out. This was that moment for us. It was the time of knowing that we were within sight of our goal, but not quite there. It was the time after a woman has prayed that someone out there can help her, even if she thinks she doesn't deserve an answer. It was the time between leaning into a kiss and feeling lips touch. I am so glad I was there to experience it.

YELLOW JESUS

When I was on a mission trip in San Herado, Ecuador, two people from the church we were visiting talked me into going all the way to Guayaquil, a three-hour journey, to look at an almost life-sized Jesus they wanted to hang in their church but could not afford. The church had just twenty members, people who walked miles on dusty roads just to get to a jar of milk.

I went to Guayaquil with an open heart, and when I arrived I saw a yellow Jesus with red paint dripping down his forehead. When I asked how much it cost, I heard the woman say in Spanish, "That will be ninety dollars." I handed her a one-hundred-dollar bill, thinking I was being generous, but she corrected me. "That will be two hundred ninety dollars," she stated, in much clearer Spanish this time.

Well, I did not want to spend that much money on a yellow Jesus, but I was way too far in it to go back on my word. So I paid the money, and they wrapped the yellow Jesus in newspaper. I carried him and his cross over my shoulder to the car and then all the way back to San Herado, grumbling to him most of the way. When I got back to San

Herado, the twenty church members loved him, and I felt a little guilty that I had complained about spending two hundred ninety dollars on Jesus.

When our group went to the little chapel later that day for a service, we found that the people had hung Jesus from an old rebar structure that had been waiting for years for him. They had tied beautiful ribbons stretching all across the church from his beautiful crown. It was humbling and amazing to see him transformed from the crucified Christ into a prince.

M&Ms IN A
BOARD MEETING

I HAD TO GO TO A BOARD MEETING, AND MY BABYSITTER
had just called to say she wouldn't be able to come
and care for my eighteen-month-old son. I got what
I thought was a really great idea. "I'll just take my
son with me and stop on the way and buy some
M&Ms," I thought. "He has never had such a great
treat, and I will feed them to him one at a time
while he plays quietly under the table."

My plan worked great for about the first seven
minutes of the meeting. He was under the table
with several toys, and I had a fistful of M&Ms ready
to give to him if he got really loud. We were just
beginning to go over the budget when I experienced
the closest thing I have known to "all hell breaking
loose."

My son started screaming, and I bent down to
give him an M&M. I opened my hand and saw
what looked like a rainbow smeared with mud, all
glistening against my sweaty palm. He screamed
again. The board members stared at me as I looked
for something to wipe my hands on so I could pick
him up.

I had heard on television since I was a child that M&Ms melt in your mouth, not in your hand. "It's a lie," I thought. "M&Ms do melt in your hand, and if they have lied to me about this, what else is a lie?" I was feeling betrayed by advertisements and by a culture that says it's okay for people to lie in advertisements. I was also feeling betrayed by feminists who had said I could do it all well.

M&Ms do in fact melt really fast in your hand, especially if you are nervous. And I was in a panic, looking for something to wipe my hands on. Finally I picked up the meeting agenda and began to wipe my hands on that, apologizing to everyone.

I knew at that moment that it was time to start dismantling my illusions and that I was just going to have to make it all up. It wasn't going to work out for me to serve on a board that met when my son needed to eat real food, and so I said good-bye and left the room, holding my son.

I remember beginning to form thoughts as I headed out into the evening. "I am going to think for myself. I am going to read the Scriptures and remember that the church helped shape them. I am going to remember that the system was set up to keep the institution alive, and I am going to mother my child as I see fit."

All of us operate under illusions of grandeur about ourselves, our faith, our system, even our candy. But if we are to live faithfully, sometimes we must set aside those illusions and trust our hearts.

REST IN PEACE

WE HAD BEEN TRAVELING AROUND IRELAND FOR ALMOST two weeks. It is a country full of ruins and dead churches that speak volumes about history, beauty, and the eternal presence of God. When we reached the village of Enniscorthy, we explored the sixth-century church ruins of St. Kevin's with about twenty other tourists. The ruins covered a half mile, and for a couple of Euro dollars you could wander around with a map and figure out which ruins were which. One was a bedroom, another a chancel, another a watchtower, or was it a library? It was hard to tell because to me most ruins look like old fences, and there was nothing remarkable or different about these ruins than hundreds of others we had seen.

It was a hot afternoon, and I could hear children playing in a field, and the grass was particularly pretty in its best green, swaying in perfect rhythm to the wind. There was a tower nearby that appeared to be in mid-fall. Crumbling from its base, it seemed to be held up only by some invisible grace. Farther on I saw the church itself, which now was a pile of old rocks. Peace descended upon me as I looked at the pile. I could almost feel the

SANCTUARY

Holy Spirit at rest, basking in her state of repose. Year by year and stone by stone, this church had begun to unbuild itself, aided by wars and neglect, not to mention wind and rain. Finally, hundreds of years ago, it became what we call ruins, a term that has a kind of sad dignity. The church was left to its own devices, and now all seems well. It is as dead as an old ruined church can get, but still it speaks to the thousands of pilgrims who come every year to look at this big old pile of rocks. I whispered a prayer as I left, hoping not to disturb the spirit that seems happy to rest in peace.

A NEW SONG

MY HUSBAND IS A SONGWRITER. MY RESPECT FOR HIS work is such that I don't watch him write. Instead, every now and then I listen from another room. He has a ritual that began long before I knew him and has continued through various places and stages of our lives. This is how it worked yesterday morning:

After the kids and animals were fed, he fixed himself a cup of coffee and sat in front of his piano and began to play a familiar melodic mantra that always seems to carry his spirit to a place where he can write. I can only imagine what he looks like in that place. The sounds fill the space I am in with great peace and tenderness. It is like listening to a prelude before worship or to monks chanting evensong. Sometimes the chord progressions take him back to one of the thousand songs he has written before. Sometimes he plays a progression over and over, and it sounds like a record skipping. But sometimes like yesterday, the progression takes off and travels to an unknown place, and I can hear him push the "record" button on the cassette player, and a melody never before sung soars into the air, bringing to life a new creation that blossoms in the morning sun.

A quarter century into writing, he still sits there every day, never doubting that a new song will emerge from the infinitely fertile ground of his soul. I want to be more like that. I want to believe that every fading moon will bring a muse to whisper in my ear. Sometimes I think, sitting in the other room sipping my own coffee, that my grieving heart holds on to old familiar melodies so tightly that I don't leave room for new ones. I hold on to loved ones who have died. I want to keep my children small so that I can always hold them.

But this beautiful new melody filling the air reminds me never to grieve what has gone before. The spirit that breathed at the dawn of creation is breathing still. So I take a deep breath and set my coffee down and pick up my pencil and a scrap of paper and write what will be the closest I ever write to a hymn in praise of the Holy Spirit.

THE HUMBLE APPROACH

SAINT MARY'S CONVENT IS LOCATED ON A BLUFF OF THE beautiful Cumberland Plateau in Tennessee. I love to go there to write and spend a day or two remembering what is important and the beautiful witness the nuns have made over the past 150 years through their simple acts of loving mercy. Recently the nuns had to sell some of their prime real estate on one of the most beautiful overlooks on the bluff to an individual named Templeton, a renowned philanthropic scholar from England, who has built a fourstory library bearing his name. I decided to take an early morning walk and go see this new structure.

I asked one of the nuns about the library before I left, and she said that, even though the place had been entirely finished for almost a year, there was not yet a single book in the library. As I made my way around the final bend that marks the approach to the building, I couldn't help but notice a huge bronze statue out front, overlooking the man-made reflection pool and stone wall. As I got close I realized that the statue, which must have been nine feet tall, was of Templeton himself. He was standing as if to greet all the visitors, and in his left hand was a book. Curious to read the title, I walked up under

57

his arm, feeling really small, and craned my neck. The title was *The Humble Approach*.

I had to laugh. Here was a man who had built a four-story library with no books, named it after himself, and erected a nine-foot statue of himself carrying a book about humility. What made it so funny was that I knew I was fully capable of doing things just as ridiculous. I sit in comfort while writing about being discomforted. I hold on to what I think is mine while writing about letting go.

I will carry the image of this statue with me for the rest of my life. Whenever I take myself too seriously, I will pull it out and remember that I am made of dust and have been given the gift of life and that I need to take the humble approach.

STEP OUT OF THE WAY

THE POLICE CALLED AT THREE O'CLOCK IN THE MORNING to tell me that one of the students who had been coming to the chapel had died. Her parents, who lived in another state, had been notified an hour before and were on their way. They had asked for me to come and say prayers for their daughter before her body was removed from the dorm room.

When I got to the room, the detective escorted me in and shut the door, leaving me alone with this precious student who was already in a thick plastic body bag. The lights were bright and flat. I could tell that she had been in bed and probably had not been expecting anyone to come in. Her clothes from the day before were still in a little pile on the floor, and there were books from class on the table.

Her parents had asked me to offer her last rites. It is a beautiful, formal prayer that includes an anointing with oil. Long ago I had memorized the prayer, but after the detective shut the door and left me in the room I knew that I wasn't as prepared as I should have been. I could not find the oils, and I didn't know if I could open the body bag. I felt that she needed a much more experienced and better priest to take the first steps with her on this next part of her journey.

For a long moment I stood before her, paralyzed by my fears and inadequacies. I wanted to do the ritual well for her and for her parents, who, on a highway somewhere, were just beginning to wake up to the reality of losing their daughter. So, instead of the first prayers being for her, I decided to throw myself into the middle of it and ask God to help me.

The answer came: "Step out of the way. This is between this beautiful child and me." And so that is what I tried to do. I offered the best of what I had so that it was about them and not me. I tried to think of what was most respectful and honorable in that moment. I knew beyond a doubt that if I made any mistakes, grace would surely make up for them.

LOVE ON A CORNER

I HAD BEEN TRAVELING WITH MY CHILDREN FOR SIX weeks. Our last stop was New York, and I was feeling tired and overwhelmed. We had seen amazing things, from the Adirondack Mountains in Vermont to the Kalahari Desert in Botswana. The trip had reminded me just how fine this world is.

I've been told by an old friend that whenever I feel overwhelmed, I just need to pray for a sign and keep going. And so, as we packed up and left our hotel on West Fifty-fifth Street, that's what I was doing.

While I was getting our things together, my kids ran ahead, and by the time I caught up with them at the corner they were playing inside a giant sculpture of the word *LOVE*. The sculpture was just those four letters in solid red and blue. I remembered having seen the image on stamps, but I never had dreamed that it was just sitting on a corner to behold. As I watched my children explore the letters, it occurred to me that this was the perfect summation not just of the trip, but of my ideal of faith.

I stood there in awe and prayed my love was this big, this welcoming, this literal, this solid, this joyful. I thought back on times when I had prayed and used the word *love* but had made it seem a lot smaller and more fragile. It was beautiful to see love in front of me, representing all that is wonderful and hopeful in this world, right smack in the middle of New York on a Wednesday morning at 8:30.

TABLE FOR TWO

MY YOUNGER BROTHER, THE REVEREND GLADSTONE Stevens, a Catholic priest and professor of theology at St. Mary's Seminary in Baltimore, was home for a week visiting. My church had just added a nine o'clock service to the schedule a few weeks before, and so far only about three or four folks had been showing up for the service.

As the service began that day, I peeked around a corner and saw that the only person in the sanctuary was my brother. I decided to wait for a few more minutes, praying that someone else might show up to join us. My brother was born with a wit matched only by his impatience and intelligence. He is a conservative theologian who talks about the "good old days" as the time before Thomas Aquinas. He loves me in spite of my gaping theological holes and once refused me communion when I tried to pass as Catholic at his ordination.

I kept waiting, but no one else came. I didn't know if I could preside at the service with just the two of us. Finally, at about 9:08, I walked out and began the service. "The Lord be with you," I said. "And also with you," he replied. I was thinking, "I do not want to do this, and I am definitely not going to preach."

As the service continued, we shared readings and a couple of stories from our youth, and things began to relax. It was actually funny when we took up the offering. Then, when we started the Eucharistic prayers, I was completely overwhelmed by the beauty of the act itself. I saw during the breaking of bread that Christ was as present as either one of us and so were both our mom and dad, who had been dead for years. He and I were simply the instruments for continuing the Eucharistic story. It was one of the sweetest Eucharists I have tasted. I gave thanks that no one else had come and diffused the intimacy and tenderness of the moment.

My brother and I were like two disciples walking half-blind on our way somewhere else, when a morsel of bread parted the clouds and, with our blindness temporarily cured, we were allowed to see truth and love. I am so self-conscious sometimes that I forget to recognize the burning feeling that calls me into the presence of God, who is staring me in the face.

FADED POCKETS

I WAS STANDING IN LINE AT A COFFEEHOUSE THAT MORNING about 6:00. It was Saturday, and I was tired, and it seemed easier to drive to a store and let them make my coffee than have to make it myself. I had been working hard all week, and that morning, when my youngest wanted me to turn on a cartoon at 5:30, I had started thinking about the mountain of house-work and errands that were facing me. I just decided to leave for fifteen minutes and take cover in a cof-feehouse.

I couldn't believe it when I walked in and there were people ahead of me in line. I was just taking in the perfection of the interior of the shop and wondering if I was falling into the trap of this corporate giant, when I noticed the man standing in front of me. He looked like a carpenter, with long graying hair and old work boots. What struck me about him was that he was wearing a really old pair of jeans, and there was a big faded ring on his back pants pocket where his tobacco can must have been sitting for about twenty years. That faded ring took me back to high school in less time than it takes to say "large caramel latté."

I remembered my high school boyfriend, who was constantly dipping tobacco. I remembered how on the weekends all the way through college we used to hike and picnic on Saturdays. Then I remembered how in 1986 we rode bicycles all the way from Chattanooga past Asheville, North Carolina. We saw beautiful countryside and sunsets. We didn't have a car between us—only the bicycles and all kinds of hope about our future.

I wondered for a second where he was and let myself feel for another second how much I missed all the freedom and adventure of being single. Then, as I waited for the milk to froth on my latté and stood behind the man with the faded ring on his pocket, I let something go. No one noticed it, but the slightest weight lifted from me and flew to its final rest. I had just made peace and said goodbye to my youth.

I think that part of living a faithful life is preparing to die. It just never occurred to me that we have to bury ourselves along the way. The faded ring was the symbol of just one of the funerals.

THE CITY CEMETERY

I WAS WALKING THROUGH THE CITY CEMETERY ON Fourth Avenue in Nashville on a cold December morning. Many famous people had taken their rest in this historic place, and I was interested in walking among the markers and reading what the people's loved ones and admirers had carved into their stones for others to read.

After thirty minutes of wandering around, I realized I was drawn to headstones that were in the later stages of deterioration. I was unconsciously playing a game: the harder it was to make out what the epitaph said, the more fun it was to try and read it. Many of the stones had finally succumbed to lichens; others to a combination of wind and water. In any case, they no longer could hold the final words and thoughts of those who cared the most.

It occurred to me, to my great surprise, that I was finding peace in the realization that when God says that we return to dust, God is not kidding. Not just our bodies, but even our limestone and granite headstones return to the dust they were made from. For some reason, it took the pressure off to see that rich and important people fade into the memory of God. We don't have to worry if our mark is big enough,

or even our marker for that matter. We don't have to worry about whether the things we leave behind will last forever, because the truth that this cemetery preaches is that they won't.

Everything will rest in peace someday as part of the dirt of creation. We come from God and are returning to God; the rest is simply the journey in between. And nothing lasts forever except love itself.

LOVE RISING
FROM THE STONES

LAST WEEK IN ECUADOR, I WALKED IN THE MOST BEAU-
tifully steep woods I had ever seen. Our ragged procession of twenty, bathed in sweat and dizzied by
altitude and bright light, mounted hundreds of
steps on the way to an outdoor chapel. The steps
were marked by seven huge stones, each carved
with an image representing a sorrowful mystery of
Christ.

We walked in full silence, yearning to reach the
top of the mountain, carrying fresh memories of
love and joy like precious oils. I realized that as I
took each step, I was saying the name of someone
in prayer. I prayed for my family, my friends, people in the church, people I knew from the streets,
people from my past, saints, and babies I have baptized. The circle of prayer got wider and wider as
the endless steps continued. My eyes and heart
were overflowing with gratitude for all the love I
have known in this world.

Finally, forty-five minutes later, we reached the
stone marking the last sorrowful mystery. I looked
up to see that the stone had given way to green

moss and was crumbling. It was no longer possible to see the carved image of Jesus being crucified. The stone was literally rolling away, and Jesus was rising from the rock, as on the very first Easter morning

All the woods in my life, and all the woods in your life, teach us the truth of resurrections. They teach us that someday love will right all the wrongs of this earth. It will set the captives free, heal our blindness, make the trees clap their hands in joy, and cause people to weep at the beauty of a field of lillies. Someday the lion will lie down with the lamb. Love, more powerful and older than stone, will roll it all away.

The Ecuadorian woods sang, "Before there were stones, there was God. Before there was death, there was life. Before there was doubt, there was faith. Before there was war, there was peace. Before there was sin, there was grace."

SHARING LONELINESS

MY FAMILY WENT TO THE STATE FAIR A FEW DAYS AGO. I really love it. I love the sensory overload: smells of cotton candy, barbeque, and the petting zoo; sights on the fairway of blinking lights, spinning wheels, and women with tattooed legs; sounds of the barkers calling you to the sideshows over the background of thrilling screams, pumped-in music, and engines driving the rides.

I have gone to this fair almost every year since the ninth grade, the year I kissed a boy named Bobby on the Ferris wheel. In those years, I have gone from being dizzy and euphoric on the rides to watching everything around me clearly so that I don't lose track of my children. This year, I watched my nine-year-old son pull away and sit alone to wait for his little brother on the bench, trying to soak it all in. Just after dark, he came up to me and said, "Mom, I'm lonely here."

Even though there were thousands of people around us and I had probably spent a hundred dollars to make sure the kids were having fun, I knew that he was right. If you let yourself really see and feel it, the fair is lonely. I gave him a hug, imagining the long path he was going to travel and all the fairs he would endure as he tried to figure out what it means to be alive in this world.

He could see beyond the lights and hear more than the loud music. He could see the man with gray hair sweeping up behind the teens who had thrown cigarette butts on the pavement. He could see that it was kind of depressing for me to hand five dollars to a young man guessing ages and weights to have him tell me I look like I am in my late thirties. He could see the fragility of the feelings between two young people who were getting their names airbrushed on matching shirts in a heart that said *Forever*. He could see, maybe for the first time, the young and old, the crippled and poor, the drunk and lonely, all thrown together with every sort and condition of person, riding in bumper cars, shooting hoops, eating peanuts.

The fair reminds me of all the spinning wheels in my life. When we are gifted with seeing them, we know there is sadness, but we can still enjoy the ride. I pray that my son, though he may feel lonely at the fair, will understand that there are whole communities of people who will ride with him.

SURRENDERING TO FLIGHT

THE IMAGE OF CHRIST ASCENDING FILLS OUR MINDS with ideas of hope, glory, and inspiration. With arms outstretched in a glowing white robe, the figure rises on a cumulus pedestal, cloaked in golden glory against a brilliant sky, saying, "I am going back to God to prepare a place for you." I love imagining this scene when I think about how it is that we are ever going to find our way home after death.

So, for practice last week, I went to the top of Bald Eagle Mountain, a beautiful place to imagine that one can fly. I stretched my arms wide in prayer and lifted my head toward the heavens. I was looking for inspiration in beatific images; what I got was a stormy, threatening nimbus cloud. I began to think of all the things I haven't done, of how in my life I have not surrendered to or been convicted in my beliefs. The feeling was not about doubts. I have come to terms with the fact that all of us mumble through different parts of the creed at different times, that we take issue with doctrines of salvation or specific beliefs about baptism and scripture. I honor all of those questions and cloudy visions. What poured concrete into my soul was knowing all of it—the scripture, the saints, the loving communities—and still being unconvicted in some way.

The saints and heroes I love are people who learned that flight comes from surrendering yourself. From Paul onward, their ascension began in losing themselves to something greater and then being unflinching in their dedication to the love of God. They faced anger and violence with truth as their armor and with arms outstretched. And on the journey they learned to fly.

Jim Zwerg was a man who could teach us to ascend. He understood that being free had to do with living out justice. During the Civil Rights movement, there was a series of bus trips called Freedom Rides. At the end of the Freedom Ride from Albany to Birmingham, there was a mob waiting, ready for blood. There were about twenty African American and white students who, when they got off the bus, were filled with terror at the prospect of facing the hatred and anger outside. Jim went first. He took some terrible blows for a greater love, and his soul ascended to a place many of us will never know.

People like Jim don't feel the need to hold onto themselves. They ascend mountains by going where they don't know the way. They inspire us to love and to live more convicted lives. If I want to fly, my faith must lift me to a new place to which I can't think my way. It must call me to a lightness of being where all things are possible and where, in the dance with truth, I can let another lead.

PARADISE FOUND

A FEW YEARS AGO MY HUSBAND AND I WENT TO HAWAII to perform a wedding ceremony for friends and, consequently, had five days alone without distractions or children. We spent hours on a perfect beach, next to a cove where sea turtles swam freely.

Sitting on the beach, I wondered if this was paradise. Was paradise a place of singing birds and guava scents, tropical plants and tangled vines draped in multi-colored flowers, all emerging from the crystal blue ocean? Perhaps paradise was really below the surface of the waters surrounding the island, in magical reefs filled with exotic colorful fish and huge green sea turtles. Perhaps paradise was simply enjoying perfectly prepared sausages and mahimahi while sipping Kona coffee and breathing in pure sky.

I decided that paradise is elusive. As soon as we name it, it is gone. It is no more realistic imagining a physical paradise than thinking there exists a place where injustice begins or happiness ends. Paradise is that wonderful memory in our souls that we have longed for since Eden. It is the promise of our hearts that we will enter a heaven laid with golden streets and singing angels. It is the tears we shed, knowing that love is being made perfect.

Every now and then we are gifted with a kiss that is different from the thousands of kisses we have kissed before, and we know that, for a moment, we are standing on the edge of paradise. On the island that day, I think I found a paradise in the deep pool of my husband's eyes, and I saw him as God sees him. I found it in colorful images as my dreams blurred into my waking. And I found it in his tender arms that, pulling me close, brought me closer to God. I believe there is a possibility that one day, many tears, years, and laughs later, I might look back and realize that in my marriage a place of paradise was found.

THE HOLY PLASTIC CUP

ABOUT A HUNDRED MEMBERS OF THE MAGDALENE community and St. Augustine's Chapel went on a retreat to Camp Nakanawa, in the hills of East Tennessee. On Saturday night we held a dance in the tiki hut, which was billed as the largest traditional tiki hut in all of America. I wondered how they actually knew that. But it did have thirteen sides and was big enough for us to string lights and dance for several hours to music from the eighties.

I really didn't think about how wonderful the dance had been until we gathered again the next morning for formal prayer and communion. The night before we had all been jumping around and drinking punch and laughing; but this morning, as we began to pray, I felt as if we were all stuck in our usual roles again, and I ached for the freedom I hadn't even known I had felt the night before. Dancing in the tiki hut, I had forgotten that I was white and forty and a mother. I didn't remember categorizing anyone else. I was learning dance moves and spinning with friends in the haloed light of Chinese lanterns. Just for a couple of hours I was lost in something bigger than me, and it was so much fun.

So, just as communion was beginning, I picked up one of the plastic cups that had held punch the night before and silently toasted our loving, dancing host and gave thanks for every time I have ever forgotten who I am. What a benevolent and loving God, who lets us forget and believe that every now and then we are truly free.

A BORROWED OFFICE

I WAS STANDING IN A SMALL OFFICE WITH CLEMMIE after her son's funeral. The office was lit by a fluorescent bulb that made the place look sallow and closed-in. There were two chairs and a laminated desk that was peeling. The walls were a dingy off-white. The room reflected the mood of the day: sad and broken.

I had known Clemmie for almost four years. She was a loving and compassionate mother. Her son, Rodriguez, was the victim of a senseless homicide in the middle of the night, in which one African American youth shot another African American youth he didn't even know.

Rodriguez had been born when Clemmie was only thirteen years old. Both of them had been in and out of the prison system. Mother and son had spoken at Magdalene's fund-raiser the previous year to talk about finding strength together in their journey toward wholeness. Now, nine months later, Clemmie and I were standing in a borrowed office after burying her only child.

We exchanged thoughts and feelings about the day. Clemmie said, "I wish I could talk to the boy who shot my son. I want to hug him for a long time and tell him I forgive him. I know that he will probably spend the rest of his life in prison, but I want him to know that God has not abandoned him."

When you tell people that you would never kill somebody, they often ask, "What if someone killed your child?" Clemmie answered the question as beautifully as I have ever heard. She had suffered more for her faith than even a martyr; she had suffered the death of her son and survived to love the enemy. I asked her if she would offer a prayer, and we knelt together in front of the desk in the sacred space that love had created.

A SLIVER OF HOPE

I HAD BEEN DRIVING OUT IN THE COUNTRY FOR ALMOST an hour when I came upon a sign that read *Craggy Hope*. The name itself sounded to me like it should be a place with just a sliver of light, like a speck of hope peeking through grey and lifeless rock.

What was stunning as I crested the hill was how the scene in front of me mirrored the image the words were conjuring in my head. It was a cold day and the land was full grey from the exposed limestone that made it poor country for farming. There were three old buzzards sitting in a barren hackberry tree on my left, and a cabin by the road had a worn-out rebel flag hanging from the clothesline near a bunch of trash and old tires.

Across the road was a fenced-in field with just one sheep standing there looking abandoned and alone. I couldn't help thinking about the gospel in which Jesus left the ninety-nine sheep to go find the one. It seemed from my vantage point that Jesus could easily have forgotten about this one forsaken sheep.

I stopped the car and took it all in. I started thinking about how many people looked like that sheep to me. People I had seen on the streets or in

jail or even in the back corner of some church, almost daring someone to offer them a hand. I have always been drawn to the single sheep. It calls me in and scares me to death. I think that is the place where we realize that Jesus seeks us out. but it is also the place of true loneliness where we feel forsaken.

I hate that place, but I cannot turn away from it. It is closer to home than I want to admit. Maybe the places that embody our fear and make the hair stick up on the backs of our necks are the ones to seek. Maybe instead of dwelling in beautiful and safe chapels, more people ought to drive until they get lost and the landscape looks abandoned and they feel what it is to be alone. Maybe then we will know how wonderful it is to have even a small sliver of light slip through the rocks and light a path wide enough for a lost sheep to follow.

MIDNIGHT

LAST NIGHT WAS ONE OF THOSE NIGHTS OF BEING AWAKE and thinking about the whole world. My mind went back to the good old days, when pajamas were still made from flammable polyester blends. My sister and I would put our pajamas into the dryer and take them out, still warm, right before bed. Then we would snuggle underneath our washable polyester comforters After our mom came in and said good night and turned off the lights, we would lift our blankets off the pajamas and watch the dancing static-electrical sparks fly. The crackling sparks made patterns like sparklers as the comforter would rise and fall. It was a cheap light show, a new invention that no one else would ever figure out.

I still love lying in bed at night and thinking of a more magical world. A world where ideas fly like sparks and what I believe is dictated by my heart. A world where the business and politics of the day work themselves out. Night thinking is clearer thinking, when dreams of a place where all the children could be fed seem plausible. It is the time to sort out things, such as what is the right thing to do and how do we really want to live and die.

MIDNIGHT

The midnight hour is the time for spiritual truth. It is the time when Martin Luther King Jr. received a vision over a cup of coffee, which gave him the resolve to speak truth with courage, even as people were planning to bomb his house. It is the time when false peace is interrupted by the consequences of fate. It is the time when the heart whispers to the head and when Christ walks on the water and rises from the dead. It is the time when strange flowers bloom for bats and when fear cloaks itself in worry. It is the time when our secrets can dance like ghosts. It is the time when prisoners are executed and captives are released. It is the time before everything, even before our prayers.

Last night I lay in bed gazing into the darkness, looking for sparks.

A RED RIBBON

YESTERDAY I SAW THE MOST AMAZING CHRISTMAS DECO-
ration on a small chipped-stucco house catty-
cornered from the Magdalene residence we are
building. The residence is on a street that is literally and symbolically a dead end.

The small stucco house has boarded windows, a
broken screen door, and a mud pit for a yard. It
exudes the feeling that, when you drive by,
inescapable and swift violence will swoop down on
you like a buzzard if you dare to slow down.

The dead-end street feels a little like the manifes-
tation of all the past and present wrongs done in
this city. Each time I go there, guys group and hover
to see if I am in the market to buy something from
them. There seem to be endless waves of racism
still rippling just under the surface, and it reminds
me that I have been a participant every time I have
turned away from that street because of fear, igno-
rance, greed, or laziness. For the past four months,
though, friends of mine and I have been going and
picking up trash, mowing the property, and trying
to learn more about our neighbors.

And then, magically, yesterday morning, a single
red ribbon appeared on the front door behind the

broken screen of the stucco house. The ribbon was the only sign of Christmas visible from our property, and it seemed humble, honest, and somehow hopeful.

For me, the ribbon was tied to a childhood song that I had all but forgotten, except for the distant memory of my mother sitting by my bed and almost whispering, "Scarlet ribbons, scarlet ribbons for her hair." I remember her shaky voice singing about a little girl who prays for scarlet ribbons for her hair. The mother goes out into the night to buy the ribbons and finds that no shops are open, so she prepares to deal with her daughter's heartbreak. But then, miraculously, the next morning the scarlet ribbons appear at the foot of the bed. I always felt like crying at the tenderness of their love.

And so yesterday, as I left the Magdalene residence, I found myself humming the tune, or at least what I could remember of it. The ribbon on the door had become a sign of hope for me, like the miracle in the story.

When I went back this morning, the ribbon was gone. And just for a moment I let myself lose the Christmas spirit. I saw the street for what it was. It was not magical, just poor, and any vision of angels in the sky was blocked out by the reality of electric wires and starlings.

And then the red ribbon wove its way back into my prayers and reminded me that God, in God's unending beauty and love, can appear unexpectedly in our lives, and that the ribbon of truth can be found in passionate hearts. Just a glimpse can keep us going. The eternal love of God comes to us in brief moments, hanging on the broken doors of our lives.

THE VIEW FROM A CAVE

A FRIEND OF MINE HAS A CABIN ON 160 ACRES IN BON Aqua, Tennessee, that I can visit when I need to be quiet. Bon Aqua means "beautiful water" and describes the land well. The cabin sits along a clear running creek that comes from a cave tucked into the side of a limestone hill.

A couple of months ago I sat in the mouth of the cave and watched the world from the inside out. The cave was damp and dark and smelled like evening. I thought about the water flowing from it and wondered where it came from. I was several months pregnant with my third child, and I felt as if I were sitting in the womb of our great mother, who keeps us alive with water and air, just as I was trying to do for my baby. It was all just a complete mystery to me. I was clueless, sitting in the earth's belly, holding my belly, about matters of consequence, such as where babies come from and where we go when we die.

Eternal life is so far out of context from our understanding that explaining its meaning would be like trying to explain to this baby the meaning of marriage. Lord knows, if we could get even a tiny glimpse inside the mystery of where this water comes from, we would probably sell the water upriver and ruin the cave forever. The same must be true for eternal life. If we could figure it out, we would try to sell it and would ruin it for everyone.

The essence of eternal life's greatness and power lies in the way it can't be grasped within our three-dimensional thinking. So I am not going to worry about it. Instead, I am going to trust the water's path that has brought me this far and trust that God will let the water carry me where it needs to after I die. If that means that my body returns to the dirt after death, I welcome it. I would be honored to be buried near Bon Aqua in the hills of Tennessee and have my heart become fertilizer for a black-eyed Susan that one day might catch the eye of a tired mother of three who is driving by and cause her to recognize the blooming plant as evidence of God's spirit. And if, instead, the river carries me to the heavens and I grow wings and have a sense of myself and see my mother and meet my Lord, I will dance a jig and celebrate with the throngs of angels at God's feet.

NOTHING IS GOING ON

I HAVE SPENT TWENTY-ONE OF THE LAST THIRTY-FIVE hours sitting in the Atlanta airport. I have lost track of where I am or what day it is. The sound of wheeled luggage against cobbled walkways reminds me of horse hooves in a Western town. Groups in gates appear to me like Athenians at the Acropolis. Security lines could easily place me in South Africa during apartheid. But mostly I feel like an omnipotent god, sitting in crowds and watching and listening with great compassion as lives pass before me.

When I first sat down, a skycap told me about wheeling an old and frail woman to the gate before I had arrived. He said he knew she felt really bad and told her he was praying for her. A few minutes later she slumped in her seat and died. He had been her priest, administering last rites. Ever since he told me this, I have been hearing the cacophony of noise and people as a chorus of love poems. People walk alone and sit alone but seem completely open to their fellow travelers. All the sermons I have ever preached about seeing Christ in others are flooding over me, and for whole minutes I feel as if I'm swimming in a sea of Christ faces.

A woman places a phone call, explains in an irritated tone that she isn't going to make it home, and rattles off a list of to-dos. Finally she says, "I wish I were home." In spite of having enough stress to weigh down any saint, she still finds the strength to speak her heart. A young man hugs his companion as she sleeps on his shoulder. A couple with a young baby hold the sleeping infant for the better part of the night, memorizing the arch of her brows. Two grey-haired women in capri pants and wild beach hats hurry by, nearly skipping.

Next to me a man says into his phone, "Nothing is going on," and I almost laugh. God must be dizzy with all the life in just this one place and all the prayers circling the satellites. There are simultaneous prayers for weddings, deaths, births, the big break, weather, a new start, and safe travels. As people turn off their cell phones to board the plane, I can almost imagine that even if the very worst happens to the plane, our collective last thought will be not about career paths or thoughts of tomorrow, but simply an overwhelming love that lifts our hearts from our chests. It's all part of a hymn we sing to God, saying, "I love you, too."

A FUNERAL PARADE

IT WAS TEN O'CLOCK ON A BEAUTIFUL SUMMER DAY TWO days after my mom's death. She was sixty-two and had been in great health, but she had contracted a rare disease that took her last breath, and now she was dead.

Mom had always said she wanted to be buried the first day after her death. But she had died at sunset and we couldn't organize the funeral in just twelve hours, so it was now the second day. We put two big pots of sunflowers in front of the biggest Episcopal church we could find, asked my husband to sing a couple of songs, asked the bishop to say some words, and put a small notice in the paper. Also in the paper was a small article about her, saying that she had raised lots of money and helped lots of people. It described her as a widow who had brought up five children while serving as the executive director of St. Luke's Community Center. What they left out was that her inheritance to her children consisted of a collection of macaroni necklaces, great stories about growing up on a farm in New York, and a house that had not changed since her children were little. She also left a legacy of forgiveness, a love of bugs, and a desire to root for the underdog.

My family and I dressed at 9:00, got to the church by 9:45, and sat down in the front row of pews as the music began. About twenty minutes into the service I noticed how many voices were singing the hymns. I looked around and was stunned to see the place over-flowing with people, so many that they were lining the walls and standing in the back. I couldn't figure out where all these folks were coming from—probably a thousand of them, coming to say thank you to a widow who never forgot to look out for the most vulnerable in our community. If these people represented even a tenth of those who were touched by her, she had lived a wonderful and rich life.

I sat there, basking in the glow of her love until the time of communion. It was then that the parade began, as each of the thousand people walked up the aisle to receive a bit of bread and wine and give thanks for the life and ministry of Anne Stevens. There appeared to be people of every age, every race, every economic class, every profession, and every sort and condition of humanity.

Watching them, I wept. I wept for the beauty of the moment, for the life it took to orchestrate this parade, and for the God who made the day exactly as she would have wanted it.

THE COLONIAL
BREAD FACTORY

THERE IS NOTHING THAT CAN COMPARE TO THE SMELL OF the old Colonial Bread factory. It was sheer coincidence that I was driving past it just as I was thinking about the week's Gospel reading in which Jesus referred to himself as the bread of life. Lost in thought, I approached the factory in the midsummer heat, just as the white smoke was filling the air with the aroma of warm yeast and sugar.

No matter how harried I am, the wafting fragrance of baking dough fills my heart with a warm, nurturing sensation. It's certainly not because of the scenery; the forty-year-old factory resides in a space of strip-mall mentality. It is a part of town where pawn shops have gone awry, and businesses specializing in large quantities of cheap merchandise flourish. The factory is surrounded by blacktop, telephone poles, and tacky orange and yellow signs claiming the cheapest loans, the best loans for cars, and green stamp trade-ins. And yet, wafting through the scene is the fragrance of baking bread in mid-rise. I swear the bread of heaven must smell just like it.

The smell of bread is an old, wonderful smell that

transports us into the realm of the holy. It is the scent of sweetness in which you think a strong bitterness would linger. It is the stuff that inspires us to keep going, even when the world looks a little run-down. Bread is the symbol of our feast at the heavenly banquet.

I laugh as I drive, thinking of the possibility that angels serve Colonial Bread made right here in a dingy part of town. To me, passing this old bread factory is like hearing Moses call out, "Let this smell of bread be a sign of hope and promise for you. Hang on and you will cross into the promised land someday, and there you will feast on bread that will taste of honey, and there will be enough for everybody!"

A TRINITY OF BEGGARS

IT WAS ST. AUGUSTINE CHAPEL'S FOURTH TRIP TO
Ecuador. We had just finished running a medical
clinic for three days and had driven through the
Andes into the beautiful city of Quenca, a Spanish
town built on Inca ruins.

As we drove along the cobbled streets, we saw
blue-and-gold domes in the distance, silhouetted
against the clear sky. It was a massive cathedral
that covered two city blocks. When we went inside,
we saw that red, brown, and white polished marble
formed the floors, walls, and endless columns. The
side chapels were dark and adorned with flowers,
prayer candles, and railings for the steady stream of
pilgrims. The moldings and statuary were a testi-
mony to the lifetimes spent on their creation.
Feeling like Dorothy entering Oz, we slowly walked
down the long aisle toward the main altar, a four-
story golden canopy surrounding a suspended marble crucifix.

In order to enter this magnificent palace we had
had to climb up four dirty, graying steps that were
worn and crooked. On two of the steps were
beggars: a blind hunched man and a frail woman
who was precariously balanced in a wheel chair with

her leg extended. As we stepped around them into the cathedral, we saw a third beggar just inside who had deep ravines cutting paths on his leather skin. Squatting, he held a small plastic bowl with a couple of coins in it. He was not begging; he was chanting as he rattled the bowl, words that, although indecipherable, carried the unmistakable message: "The poor will always be with you."

Wherever we walked within the great tomblike church, we could hear the echo of the beggar's voice. As we sat and watched an old man kneel at the foot of a porcelain Magdalene, or watched a tired young mother with a baby bundled on her back cross herself to the Virgin, we could hear it: "The poor will always be with you."

Hearing the beggar's chant in my ear, it occurred to me that I had almost missed God. Although I could see the cathedral as beautiful, it was hard for me to see the trinity of beggars as beautiful. I had compassion for them, I could give to them, but I couldn't see them as beautiful. It was hard to smell their sweat as incense, hard to think about their tragic stories as lavish soil for humility and truth, hard to take in the canyon-sized crater of need as a container for endless mercy. And until we can, we will miss the Lord every time.

SANCTUARY

For a moment in Quenca I felt God's presence. He was on the steps of the cathedral, chanting with the beggar. Inside, we were not worshiping with the living God who is hard to look upon. We were just genuflecting the likeness of him in stone. The proclamation "The poor will always be with you" is not a curse, but a blessing. If we want to see God, we simply need to keep giving the thirsty a drink, housing the poor, going to respite, comforting those who weep, tending the sick, anointing and burying the dead, and seeing it all as beautiful.

THERE IS NO PLACE
THAT GOD IS NOT

PEGGY SUE DIED LAST WEEK. I MET HER THROUGH LISA, a graduate of Magdalene and an old friend, who had called me and asked if I would go to the hospital to visit a woman she knew.

Three years ago Peggy Sue had been a baker. She became addicted to crack and, after living between the streets and jail, was now dying from AIDS and syphilis under state custody at General Hospital. When I met her she weighed eighty-five pounds and looked as if her body were bearing the sickness of the whole world. She knew scripture and would tell me about her life and then ask me please to take her home with me.

When Peggy Sue died, she was in an amazing state of peace despite the sickness and the prison guards at her door. I imagine that if Elijah's chariot was coming to bring somebody home, it was for her. She needed to get there quick.

The state put her ashes in a cardboard box and gave us fifteen minutes at a local funeral home with a boom box and a choice of songs. A wilting flower sat by the ashes. A group of us gathered together, and as we began the first prayer I thought, "This has got to be the worst that life can offer and the most depressing funeral possible. God must be as far away as Pluto." But as I finished the thought I realized that all of us standing together were overcome with emotion. God's presence was filling the room, which contained nothing else.

As we prayed I had a vision of Peggy Sue lying in repose on Jesus' lap. He was holding her close because she had been hurting for so long, starving outside the vineyard, while many of us drank the wine. In my vision Jesus was weeping, not for Peggy Sue, but for the rest of us who still suffer.

WAITING FOR A HORSE

HORSES CARRY THE SPIRIT OF GOD IN THEIR GAIT. IT IS always magical to watch a horse run and see its mane dancing free in the wind.

The other day a friend of mine invited me to come to her farm to sit and watch her horses run free in their huge pasture. I chose a particularly lovely day, bought the best cup of coffee I could find, and found a quiet spot near a stone fence with a stand of trees nearby. The scene was set, with surround-sound crickets and the kind of slow-motion clouds that make you believe you have all the time in the world.

I sat in silence and waited. Then I started to get fidgety. I realized I had to be somewhere in an hour. Furthermore, even though I could hear the horses neighing every now and then, I hadn't actually seen one. They needed to come out so that I could see them as a witness to the living spirit of God, and so that my morning of inspiration wasn't wasted.

I listened for the horses. Thinking I heard them running, I started down into a thick stand of trees. They weren't there. I thought, *This isn't getting me anywhere. I wish I had some trick to make them come running toward me.*

Standing there near the edge of the trees, itchy and impatient, I finally came to myself and found the humor of my situation. I am in a bad way when I start approaching the Spirit as if I'm on a game hunt. Better for it to stay hidden than to waste its meaning on a wretched soul who is trying to use it like a commodity.

I sat there alone with no signs, just the dead still of the morning as my guide. I waited until I was done with the lesson, then wiped the grass stains off my rear, poured out my cold coffee, and headed back toward the car.

As I walked, I apologized to God for all the times I had gone to church to hear myself speak and for carrying the silly notion that I could ever schedule God's spirit to move in my life. I apologized to the horses, wherever they were, for thinking a novice could look at them and have any idea how beautiful they were.

I climbed into the car and drove to the stables, where I found my friend. "How was your morning?" she asked.

"Perfect," I said. And I meant it.

A POOR CATHEDRAL

ON A TUESDAY MORNING IN NEW YORK CITY, AFTER stuffing ourselves with Peking duck the night before, my husband and I walked down to see St. Joseph's and St. Mary's houses of hospitality.

These houses of hospitality opened in 1932, when Dorothy Day and Peter Maurin offered soup and bread to long lines of poor people during the Depression. Starting with about twenty dollars in donations and a paper that they sold for one cent a copy, Day and Maurin bought a big kettle, some ingredients, and a few loaves of bread. They lived in poverty and invited others to join them as they kept the soup on, served the hungry, and awakened the social consciousness of church men and women in this country.

When my husband and I got to St. Joseph's at 9:30, there were thirty people in line for soup. Each person had that layered-in-dirty-clothes-with-a-sack-in-each-hand look of the chronic homeless. We waited until the doors opened at 10:00. A young man, face without a wrinkle, wearing wire-rimmed glasses, his last haircut just a memory, looking full of idealism, invited us to come in and apologized for the way everything looked.

Inside, the whole scene was beautifully familiar, like every community center or soup kitchen I have ever worked in: everyone crammed together, trying to work in a building too small and too run-down to accommodate the ever-growing needs of the oppressed.

"There isn't much to see," said the young man, "but try going up to Fifth Street to the women's building where the chapel is, where Dorothy worshiped for decades."

We made our pilgrimage to St. Mary's, and a young woman named Christie welcomed us and directed us to the chapel. It was a musty, old, small dark room, lit by a single candle for the leftover bread and wine. There was a thick, long, natural wooden altar at the front with fold-out chairs for seats. Behind the altar hung a picture of thirteen dark, unrecognizable faces in a circle.

It was one of the most beautiful chapels I have ever seen because of what was not there. The workers at the house never built a big memorial or a beautiful church dedicated to Dorothy Day; instead they have kept the soup cooking for over seventy years and have fed hundreds of thousands of people. The people have been fed through depressions and prosperity, through peace and war. I was humbled in that space and reminded of the importance of renewing a right spirit within me.

THE FOOD CHAIN

THERE WAS A BEAUTIFUL COMBINATION OF JEWELWEED and southern asters just off the highway. For me, fields of wildflowers are always like calling cards for the Spirit, and so I pulled onto a small side road to sit on the hood of my car and breathe them in for just a little bit.

It was during a pause in the highway sounds that I first heard the angry crow. His cries appeared to be coming from a stand of trees that began about a hundred yards past the field of wildflowers. Then I heard what sounded like a wounded cry. I couldn't imagine what was happening. I decided to abandon the car and go closer. I was in the middle of a muddy field when I saw what was happening. The crow was attacking a hawk that every now and then made that horrible wounded cry. The hawk came around, and the crow, making his war cry, bit him again. Then the hawk flew off but soon circled to try and come back once again.

I wondered how long this game of cat and mouse had been going on, and I realized that the answer was forever. The hawk is chased by the crow that is chased by the mockingbird that is chased by the blue jay that is chased by the squirrel. It was probably a squirrel that this hawk was chasing, which made the circle complete. Ever since I have known to keep an eye out, I have seen people chasing each other, and I know that I am well inside that circle myself. I chase after whatever I think I can catch and hope that whatever is after me won't catch up.

The hawk started to fly off again, but this time the crow kept on his tail. The crow didn't realize that he would never catch the hawk; he would only keep the chase going until the hawk finally lost interest. I hope I have just about lost interest in the chase and will turn around and see all the amazing things I keep running away from.

HALF-MAST

I WENT WALKING ON A BEAUTIFUL FALL DAY THROUGH A
military cemetery on the outskirts of town. I was
actually trying to find a hiking trail but got lost and
ended up there by mistake. I loved the idea, looking
at the fall colors, that it was possible for a cemetery
to be in uniform. The cemetery took up several hill-
sides, and I thought I could walk around in there
for a while before I headed back into town.

As I was walking through endless rows, reading
names, wars, and ranks, I noticed two gravediggers
standing about twenty rows away. They were leaning against a marker in a sea of markers, smoking
cigarettes by the six-foot hole they had just dug,
and were waiting for the hearse. The backhoe was
parked nearby, and their shovels had been thrown
to the ground.

I was curious about what was unfolding in front
of me and decided to sit and watch the service and
offer my own prayers. A few minutes later the
hearse pulled up. The gravediggers took their last
puffs and threw their cigarette butts near the hole.
A couple of people driving the hearse helped get the
casket on rollers, and then, with no ceremony, they
began lowering the coffin into the hole.

I wanted to make my presence known; it was starting to feel like an emergency to me. I wanted to call out to those guys, "Wait, I'm a priest; I can read some scripture and say a prayer." But I felt like an eavesdropper and thought it best to stay back and offer a silent prayer. And without thinking, one of the first prayers that formed in my mind was, "God, please don't let me be buried like this."

An old friend once told me that during funeral services, everyone imagines their own funeral. I bet this wasn't the funeral imagined by the man who was being buried. I bet he thought they would put the flag at half-mast, and a group would be seated in some velvet chairs, and a woman in black would clutch a flag folded in a triangle to her bosom. I began to feel, crouched between the graves of World War II vets, that somehow this ceremony would depress him and he would feel abandoned.

Just as I was about to pronounce the whole thing a failure, a beautiful red-tailed hawk cut a path above us, and its shadow, shaped like an eagle, passed over his fresh grave. And I remembered how it is never my place, or anyone's place, to call anything a failure. It is God's world and God's holy ground, and it is sacred.

NEW MOON

IT WAS ONE CF THE DARKEST NIGHTS I HAD SEEN FOR A while. I had been sitting on the porch, hoping for the moon to rise and lift my spirits with her bright and shining face. There is a reason the greatest poets, prophets, and lovers look to the moon for inspiration. It is the unifying vision of our earth. We all can look at the moon from wherever we are and rest assured that those we love can look up and see the same moon.

I remember when I took my first trip overseas alone and saw the moon from a train window. It brought me great comfort to know that my mom could see that same beautiful full moon. The moon that lonely night was big enough that it seemed to hold the face of all humanity. I imagined my mom seeing my face in its reflection as she looked up that night. Then once, years later, I remember nursing my child in the middle of the night and seeing a perfect smile coming from the half-moon. There was a clear, white aura around the smile, and it brought me great peace and hope. On nights like those, I can praise sister moon with St. Francis and believe that people fall in love under her spell.

But on this night there was nothing. It was as if the moon were dressed in flannel-gray clouds and had called it a night. She was hiding her face from

everyone who was looking to her for assurance. Now it seemed that my prayers would drift to the heavens, slip past the sleeping moon, and meander through the night with no destination. I continued to sit there until finally my thoughts hit bottom and I thought the worst: there is no God. Our prayers do not travel from our lips to God's ears. They simply go out past Pluto into the dark night, and there is nothing else. In that moment I couldn't recall the moon's face or a single image of God. And so it was that my heart for a second faltered. Then miraculously it started to beat again.

As I began to crawl from the moon-like crater in which I found myself, I remember thinking: I can take the worst. If this is doubt, I am going to welcome it too. If the worst is sometimes thinking that this is all there is, I can live with it. I can live with just this, knowing that I have felt love. And I will carry on the next morning. I will start the coffee and open the church for business.

I left with the thought that the next day I would get up and try to love God again, and I would try and love my neighbor as myself. And then I would come back to this very spot the next night, knowing that love remained and somehow God had provided just enough light to cut a path for me till dawn.

OUTSIDE A SHOE STORE

THERE'S A SHOE STORE THAT HAS BEEN AROUND FOR thirty years on the right-hand side of the main entrance to the mall in Green Hills. It's completely glassed-in and filled with single shoes displayed along glass counters on clear shoe horns. I have never been in it. It occurred to me for the first time the other day that I could go in it. Unconsciously since childhood, that store has not been an option. I don't know if it's because it just looks expensive or because my mom's idea of new shoes was old canvas tennis shoes with a new application of white shoe polish.

Shoes were one of the first symbols I remember of priesthood. I got ordained in clogs and was kneeling in a huddle of priests laying hands on me, and when I opened my eyes for a moment I noticed I was surrounded by black shoes, mostly tasseled. I thought, "It is going to be hard to wear my shoes in this job."

Something about shoes eludes me. When I went to talk with the bishop about our desire to start a capital fund, I decided I'd better look nice. So I crossed the street to Tori "the Imelda Marcos of Nashville" Taff's house and borrowed a bone sandal with a modest heel. I got feedback later that the way I dressed hadn't helped my cause. Especially as a woman, you can't win. Women are frequently left out of the inner sanctum because of what they wear, what they say, or what they don't say, and for being too forward, too crass, too sexy, or too uptight, and end up alienated.

The homecoming queen of alienation has got to be the Canaanite woman in the Gospel of John. Like me as I stand outside the glass walls of the shoe store, the Canaanite woman waits outside the room where Jesus sits. She hesitates to go in, knowing the silence that may greet her, fearing dismissive comments such as, "Dogs shouldn't expect to eat what's meant for children." She knows that the power is not in her hands, no matter how strong hers are.

But in her desperation, because of her need for truth, wholeness, health, and freedom, she moves beyond the glass walls. Out of her great courage, she encourages us to stand in our shoes when we are outside the inner sanctum, under the glass ceiling. She crosses political, social, and religious barriers and proclaims the gift of intimacy with God. She is a hero who stands toe-to-toe with the Lord, celebrating the freedom that her otherness gives her to speak the truth and plead her case.

She speaks to all of us, male and female, in our otherness in this world. I do not know what it is to be Iraqi or African American or gay or blind or to have a criminal record, but I do know a little of my otherness, and the Canaanite woman makes me thankful for it. The otherness is the place through which we find our way to God. In filling our shoes, we make strange tracks, but that is the path we walk to holiness. In that walk, new gospel is written, love is discovered, and lives are saved.

I stand outside the shoe store. For the first time, I walk inside.

IT'S ALL A GIFT

ON THE FIRST DAY OF A TRIP TO THE GRAND TETONS, I took my two youngest boys to a place called Two Oceans Lake. It was a shiny day. Everything was sparkling and beautiful: the lake, the clear blue sky, and my hopes of frolicking in the woods with my boys.

About three miles into the four-mile loop, my youngest was sound asleep on my back, so I asked my six-year-old to be really quiet. It was truly a moment of peace. Then, as we came around a corner, we saw a grizzly bear standing not more than fifteen feet away. The bear turned and faced us on the trail, and in that instant everything changed. Peace transformed into dread. It filled my body like concrete as I prayed for the bear to kill me, not my kids. I didn't see how to get out of it.

I walked slowly backwards, and my six-year-old started to cry. The bear took a couple of steps toward us. Ripples moved from its shoulders to its paws, and we saw the golden outline of its eyes. I felt a hiccup coming on and tried to suppress it.

I rounded a corner on the trail. The bear could no

longer see me. And my feelings changed again. As soon as I decided the grizzly had spared us, I started thinking about how wonderful my life was. I gave thanks for everything, and the only things for which I apologized were my laziness and the times when I had not spoken truth and had not loved well.

My boys and I hurried down the trail, away from the bear. About twenty minutes later a woman came from the other direction. I told her what had happened, and she assured us that the bear was certainly not a grizzly and that we could scare it away. So, with renewed confidence, accompanied by this self-assured hiker, we walked back toward the bear. As we came around that same corner, the bear turned toward us again.

"Oh, my God!" screamed the woman. "It's a grizzly!"

This time there was neither peace nor quiet thoughts; we just grabbed my sons and abandoned the trail, screaming. It took nearly ten minutes for my husband to hear us and come to help.

When we finally made it to our car, I had lost my voice, had two bruises on my shoulders from the backpack, and was shaky in my thighs. I must have said a hundred times, "The kids and I were spared twice. I will see it all as a gift."

A little later in the day, we sat outside our cabin and the sky was full of light and I was full of gratitude looking at the heavens on that beautiful, shiny day.

BENEDICTION

The sun begins the procession in a deep orange
  chasuble
as the frogs and crickets begin the opening hymn.
The thistle genuflects reverently as the leaves
  rustle to find their place.

The spring-fed lake reflects on the world,
and is ready to accept the born-again dragonflies
  that have heard the call.

The harmonies of the cardinals, sparrows,
and occasional crow offer the praise
as creation begins its communion with the moon.

And just as the sun dips beneath the shroud of trees
  that covers it
and turns the day to memory,
a barred owl calls out the benediction.

Let creation which passes all understanding,
keep your heart and mind in the knowledge and
  love of God.

Let the dirt you are made from join in the last
  chorus,
and let the water that flows through your veins
  give thanks.